The Little Book of

# WRINKLIES' WIT
# & WISDOM
*Forever!*

D0609122

First published in Great Britain in 2008 by Prion
an imprint of the Carlton Publishing Group
20 Mortimer Street
London W1T 3JW

2 4 6 8 10 9 7 5 3 1

The material in this book was previously published in
*Wrinklies' Wit & Wisdom Forever!*

A CIP record for this book is available from the British Library

ISBN 978-1-85375-653-5

Printed in Singapore

The Little Book of

# WRINKLIES' WIT
# & WISDOM
*Forever!*

Compiled by
Allison Vale & Alison Rattle

PRION

# Introduction

The wrinkly years are not
to be denied, reviled or
feared, but to be welcomed
and enjoyed. Forget a quiet,
dignified old age and
party on!

You can tell a lot about a
fellow's character by his way
of eating jellybeans.

Ronald Reagan

Women speak because they wish to speak, whereas a man speaks only when driven to speech by something outside himself – like, for instance, he can't find any clean socks.

Jean Kerr

Never kick a fresh turd on a hot day.

Harry S. Truman

It is better to waste one's youth than to do nothing with it at all.

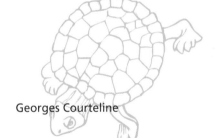

Georges Courteline

Life's under no obligation to
give us what we expect.

Margaret Mitchell

I once had a rose named after me and I was very flattered. But I was not pleased to read the description in the catalogue: no good in a bed, but fine up against a wall.

Eleanor Roosevelt

Once you can accept
the universe as matter
expanding into nothing that
is something, wearing stripes
with plaid comes easy.

Albert Einstein

I think a lot about getting old. I don't want to be one of those 70-year-olds who still want lots of sex.

Rupert Everett

For every fatal shooting, there were roughly three non-fatal shootings. And, folks, this is unacceptable in America. It's just unacceptable. And we're going to do something about it.

George W. Bush

I will not eat oysters. I want my food dead. Not sick, not wounded, dead.

Woody Allen

A new Viagra virus is going round the Internet. It doesn't affect your hard drive, but you can't minimise anything for hours.

Joan Rivers

You take your life in your
own hands and what
happens? A terrible thing:
no one to blame.

Erica Jong

It is inhumane, in my opinion, to force people who have a genuine medical need for coffee to wait in line behind people who apparently view it as some kind of recreational activity.

Dave Barry

There's a fine line between fishing and just standing on the shore like an idiot.

Steven Wright

Man invented language to satisfy his deep need to complain.

Lily Tomlin

The simple truth is that balding African-American men look cool when they shave their heads, whereas balding white men look like giant thumbs.

Dave Barry

A healthy male adult bore
consumes each year one and
a half times his own weight in
other people's patience.

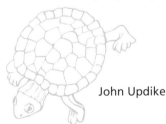

John Updike

Home computers are being called upon to perform many new functions, including the consumption of homework formerly eaten by the dog.

Doug Larson

A common mistake people make when trying to design something completely foolproof is to underestimate the ingenuity of complete fools.

Douglas Adams

As a lady of a certain age, I am willing to let the photographers and their zoom lenses stay, but only if they use their Joan Collins lens on me for close-ups.

Kay Ullrich

You don't appreciate a lot of stuff in school until you get older. Little things like being spanked every day by a middle-aged woman: stuff you pay good money for in later life.

Emo Philips

How on earth did Gandhi manage to walk so far in flip-flops? I can't last 10 minutes in mine.

Mrs. Merton

I have to be careful to get out
before I become the grotesque
caricature of a hatchet-faced
woman with big knockers.

Jamie Lee Curtis

We live in an age when pizza
gets to your home before
the police.

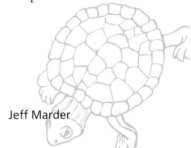

Jeff Marder

One day you look in the mirror and you realize that the face you are shaving is your father's.

Robert Harris

Each has his past shut in
him like the leaves of a book
known to him by his heart
and his friends can only read
the title.

Virginia Woolf

A hospital bed is a parked taxi, with the meter running.

Groucho Marx

The good news about mid-life is that the glass is still half-full. Of course, the bad news is that it won't be long before your teeth are floating in it.

Anon

Fishing is boring, unless you catch an actual fish, and then it is disgusting.

Dave Barry

Sex and golf are the two things you can enjoy even if you're not good at them.

Kevin Costner

I like men who have a future
and women who have a past.

Oscar Wilde

A plastic surgeon's office is the only place where no one gets offended when you pick your nose.

MAD Magazine

Was it you or your brother
who was killed in the war?

Rev. William Spooner

Golf: a game where white men can dress up as black pimps and get away with it.

Robin Williams

The scientific theory I like
best is that the rings of Saturn
are composed entirely of lost
airline luggage.

Mark Russell

I am really looking forward,
as I get older and older, to
being less and less nice.

**Annette Bening**

We look forward to a
disorderly, vigorous,
unhonoured and disreputable
old age.

Don Marquis

If women dressed for men,
the stores wouldn't sell much
– just an occasional sun visor.

Groucho Marx

The thing you realize as you get older is that parents don't know what the hell they're doing and neither will you when you get to be a parent.

Mark Hoppus

If it weren't for electricity,
we'd all be watching
television by candlelight.

George Gobel

We are living in a world
today where lemonade is
made from artificial flavours
and furniture polish is made
from real lemons.

Alfred E. Newman

The Devil himself had probably re-designed Hell in the light of information he had gained from observing airport layouts.

Anthony Price

I can win an argument on any topic, against any opponent. People know this and steer clear of me at parties. Often, as a sign of their great respect, they don't even invite me.

Dave Barry

I don't think kids have a problem with death. It's us older ones who are nearer to it that start being frightened.

Helena Bonham Carter

The older we grow the greater becomes our wonder at how much ignorance one can contain without bursting one's clothes.

Mark Twain

It was a bold man who first
swallowed an oyster.

Jonathan Swift

Abortion is advocated
only by persons who have
themselves been born.

Ronald Reagan

If I stop at a zebra crossing,
I stop and wave, and I'd like
them to wave. But if they
don't, then I think, 'Well, you
bastard, this is the last time
I'm gonna do this for you.'


**Don Warrington**

My wife and I tried to breakfast together, but we had to stop or our marriage would have been wrecked.

Winston Churchill

The thing with high-tech is
that you always end up
using scissors.

David Hockney

My wallpaper and I are
fighting a duel to the death.
One or the other of us has
to go.

Oscar Wilde

The old believe everything;
the middle-aged
suspect everything;
the young know everything.

Oscar Wilde

I would like to find a stew that will give me heartburn immediately, instead of at three o'clock in the morning.

John Barrymore

For my sister's 50th birthday, I sent her a singing mammogram.

Steven Wright

It is not all bad, this getting old, ripening. After the fruit has got its growth it should juice up and mellow. God forbid I should live long enough to ferment and rot, and fall to the ground in a squash.

Emily Carr

I was so naive as a kid I used to sneak behind the barn and do nothing.

Johnny Carson

Computers are useless. They can only give you answers.

Pablo Picasso

Never pick a fight with an ugly person. They've got nothing to lose.

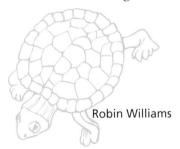

Robin Williams

Nothing goes out of fashion
sooner than a long dress with
a very low neck.

Coco Chanel

The problem with beauty is
that it's like being born rich
and getting poorer.

Joan Collins

I am not the first man who wanted to make changes in his life at 60 and I won't be the last. It is just that others can do it with anonymity.

Harrison Ford

What do I know of man's destiny? I could tell you more about radishes.

Samuel Beckett

Don't worry about the world coming to an end today. It's already tomorrow in Australia.

Charles M. Schulz

The seven dwarves of menopause: itchy, bitchy, sweaty, sleepy, bloated, forgetful and psycho.

Anon

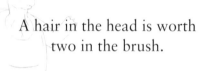

A hair in the head is worth
two in the brush.

Don Herold

It is after you have lost your teeth that you can afford to buy steaks.

Pierre Auguste Renoir

Show me a man with both
feet on the ground and I'll
show you a man who can't
get his pants on.

Joe E. Lewis

When a man retires, his wife gets twice the husband, but only half the income.

Chi Chi Rodriguez

I am happy now that Charles calls on my bedchamber less frequently than of old. As it is, I now endure but two calls a week and when I hear his steps outside my door I lie down on my bed, close my eyes, open my legs and think of England.

Lady Alice Hillingdon

Retirement: it's nice to get out of the rat race, but you have to learn to get along with less cheese.

Gene Perret

An hour with your grandchildren can make you feel young again. Anything longer than that and you start to age quickly.

Gene Perret

I've been grumpy since the age of 10, so it wasn't a generational shift. I never expect anything to get better. I just am grumpy.

Sir Bob Geldof

When I die, bury me on the golf course so my husband will visit.

Anon

In gardens, beauty is a by-product. The main business is sex and death.

Sam Llewellyn

I hate women because
they always know where
things are.

James Thurber

It was not so long ago
that people thought
semiconductors were part-
time orchestra leaders
and microchips were very,
very small snack foods.


Geraldine Ferraro

My 50 years have shown me that few people know what they are talking about. I don't mean idiots that don't know. I mean everyone.

John Cleese

The fear of death is the most
unjustified of all fears, for
there's no risk of accident for
someone who's dead.


Albert Einstein

I do try and keep fit, but it's a half-hearted battle. I'll go for a jog once a fortnight and then feel ill for two days afterwards. And now and again I'll join a health club, but the trauma of filling in the form and having my photo taken for the membership card usually puts me off going for about 12 months. But I'm still optimistic that one day I'll be offered a guest role in *Baywatch*.

Steve Coogan

Try to keep your soul young
and quivering right up to
old age.

George Sand

Football and cookery are the
two most important subjects
in this country.

Delia Smith

Television is chewing gum for the eyes.

Frank Lloyd Wright

I would not live forever, because we should not live forever, because if we were supposed to live forever, then we would live forever, but we cannot live forever, which is why I would not live forever.

Miss Alabama,
*1994 Miss USA contest*

If women ran the world we wouldn't have wars, just intense negotiations every 28 days.

Robin Williams

Oh, I like smoking, I do. I smoke for my health, my mental health. Tobacco gives you little pauses, a rest from life. I don't suppose anyone smoking a pipe would have road rage, would they?

David Hockney

Robert Redford used to be such a handsome man and now look at him: everything has dropped, expanded and turned a funny colour.

George Best

At 65 and drawing a state pension, I was delighted to discover that only people under 45 would regard me as old, even though sadly nobody would actually call me young.

Alexander Chancellor

My formula for living is quite simple. I get up in the morning and I go to bed at night. In between, I occupy myself as best I can.

Cary Grant

Now there are more overweight people in America than average-weight people. So overweight people are now average. Which means you've met your New Year's resolution.

Jay Leno

My memory is going. I brush my teeth, and then 10 minutes later I go back and have to feel the toothbrush. Is it wet? Did I just brush them?

Terry Gilliam

Underwear makes me
uncomfortable and, besides,
my parts have to breathe.

Jean Harlow

There is only one cure for
grey hair. It was invented
by a Frenchman. It is called
the guillotine.

P.G. Wodehouse

People say fish is good for a diet. But fish should never be cooked in butter. Fish should be cooked in its natural oils – Texaco, Mobil, Exxon...

Rodney Dangerfield

If you want to look young
and thin, hang around
old fat people.

Jim Eason

I have six locks on my door all in a row. When I go out, I only lock every other one. I figure no matter how long somebody stands there picking the locks, they are always locking three.

Elayne Boosler

I don't like small birds. They hop around so merrily outside my window, looking so innocent. But I know that secretly they're watching my every move, and plotting to beat me over the head with a large steel pipe and take my shoe.

Jack Handey

You were born an original.
Don't die a copy.

John Mason

I am amazed at radio DJs today. I am firmly convinced that AM on my radio stands for Absolute Moron. I will not begin to tell you what FM stands for.

Jasper Carrott

She had so many gold teeth…
she used to have to sleep with
her head in a safe.

W.C. Fields

You can't help getting older,
but you don't have to get old.

George Burns

Male menopause is a lot more
fun than female menopause.
With female menopause
you gain weight and get hot
flushes. Male menopause –
you get to date young girls
and drive motorcycles.

Rita Rudner

I spent 90 per cent of my
money on women and drink.
The rest I wasted.

George Best

Rock journalism is people
who can't write interviewing
people who can't talk for
people who can't read.

Frank Zappa

I have the body of an 18-year-old. I keep it in the fridge.

Spike Milligan

And so, in my State of the – my State of the Union – or state – my speech to the nation, whatever you want to call it, speech to the nation – I asked Americans to give 4,000 years – 4,000 hours over the next – the rest of your life – of service to America. That's what I asked – 4,000 hours.

George W. Bush

Do not do unto others as you expect they should do unto you; their tastes may not be the same.

George Bernard Shaw

It is better to die on your feet
than to live on your knees.

Dolores Ibarruri

My secret for staying young
is good food, plenty of rest
and a make-up man with a
spray gun.

Bob Hope

I have a punishing workout regimen. Every day I do three minutes on a treadmill, then I lie down, drink a glass of vodka and smoke a cigarette.

Anthony Hopkins

If you drink, don't drive.
Don't even putt.

Dean Martin

The countryside is incredibly boring. There's lots of shagging, lots of murders, lots of sarcasm, lots of treachery and lots of bad cooking, but it's all hidden. You've got all the space and the flowers, but it's dull!

Tom Baker

My doctor gave me six months to live, but when I couldn't pay the bill he gave me six more.

Walter Matthau

When I was growing up,
there were two things that
were unpopular in my house.
One was me and the other
was my guitar.

Bruce Springsteen

Everyone says I'm terrified of getting old, but the truth is that in my job becoming old and extinct are one and the same thing.

Cher

I have left orders to be awakened at any time in case of national emergency, even if I'm in a cabinet meeting.

Ronald Reagan

I don't want to achieve immortality through my work, I want to achieve it through not dying.

Woody Allen

A woman's always younger
than a man at equal years.

Elizabeth Barrett Browning

Some people ask the secret of our long marriage. We take time to go to a restaurant two times a week. A little candlelight, dinner, soft music and dancing. She goes Tuesdays, I go Fridays.

Henny Youngman

Give a man a fish and he has food for a day. Teach him how to fish and you can get rid of him for the entire weekend.

Zenna Schaffer

Getting old is a fascination thing. The older you get, the older you want to get.

Keith Richards

I'm not ageing,
I just need re-potting.

Anon

Golf is more fun than walking naked in a strange place, but not much.

Buddy Hackett

The only real way to look younger is not to be born so soon.

Charles M. Schulz

People say that age is just a state of mind. I say it's more about the state of your body.

Geoffrey Parfitt

One of the most difficult things to contend with in a hospital is that assumption on the part of the staff that because you have lost your gall bladder you have also lost your mind.

Jean Kerr

Her own mother lived the latter years of her life in the horrible suspicion that electricity was dripping invisibly all over the house.

James Thurber

Charlotte: Listen to this: sometime in the 10 years before menopause, you may experience symptoms including all-month-long PMS, fluid retention, insomnia, depression, hot flushes or irregular periods.

Carrie: On the plus side, people start to give up their seats for you on the bus.

*Sex and the City*

I'm tired of all this nonsense about beauty being only skin-deep. That's deep enough. What do you want – an adorable pancreas?

Jean Kerr

My doctor is wonderful.
Once, in 1955, when I
couldn't afford an operation,
he touched up the x-rays.

Joey Bishop

I always wanted to be an explorer, but it seemed I was doomed to be nothing more than a very silly person.

Michael Palin

If I were reincarnated, I would wish to be returned to Earth as a killer virus to lower human population levels.

Prince Philip

How can I believe in God
when just last week I got my
tongue caught in the roller of
an electric typewriter?

Woody Allen

You can calculate Zsa Zsa
Gabor's age by the rings on
her fingers.

Bob Hope

Another possible source of guidance for teenagers is television, but television's message has always been that the need for truth, wisdom and world peace pales by comparison with the need for a toothpaste that offers whiter teeth and fresher breath.

Dave Barry

The secret of longevity is to keep breathing.

Sophie Tucker

There is a very fine line
between 'hobby' and
'mental illness'.

Dave Barry

I hate the fact that supermarkets are supposed to be open 24 hours. What that means is if you go at 10 at night, there's only one checkout open, so it takes you just as long as if you went at four o'clock in the afternoon.

Germaine Greer

I'm so old they've cancelled
my blood type.

Bob Hope

Everyone probably
thinks that I'm a raving
nymphomaniac, that I have
an insatiable sexual
appetite, when the truth is I'd
rather read a book.

Madonna

Politics:'poli', a Latin word
meaning 'many';
and 'tics' meaning
'bloodsucking creatures'.

Robin Williams

When you finally go back to your old home town, you find it wasn't the old home you missed but your childhood.

Sam Ewing

Retirement must be wonderful. I mean, you can suck in your stomach for only so long.

Burt Reynolds

My mum died about three years ago at the age of 101, and just towards the end, as she began to run out of energy, she did actually stop trying to tell me what to do most of the time.

John Cleese

I've been in love with the same woman for 49 years. If my wife ever finds out, she'll kill me.

Henny Youngman

The important thing in acting
is to be able to laugh and cry.
If I have to cry, I think of my
sex life. If I have to laugh,
I think of my sex life.

Glenda Jackson

Smokers of the world unite! We have been bullied and nannied long enough. And if Tony Blair is tempted to follow the lead of Ireland and Italy, let us remind him that only 10.7 million voted Labour last time. But 15 million smoke.

Tom Utley

The ultimate indignity is
to be given a bedpan by
a stranger who calls you
by your first name.

Maggie Kuhn

Adulthood is the ever-shrinking period between childhood and old age. It is the apparent aim of modern industrial societies to reduce this period to a minimum.

Thomas Szasz

My toughest fight was with my first wife and she won every round.

Muhammad Ali

I guess I don't so much mind
being old, as I mind being fat
and old.

Peter Gabriel

There are only two ways of telling the complete truth –
anonymously
and posthumously.

Thomas Sowell

You know you're getting old
when everything hurts.
And what doesn't hurt
doesn't work.

Hy Gardner

I don't want to retire.
I'm not that good at
crossword puzzles.

Norman Mailer

Too bad that all the people who know how to run the country are driving taxi cabs and cutting hair.

George Burns

My wife is a sex object. Every time I ask for sex, she objects.

Les Dawson

I get in a complete rage with the computer. I get all hot, my hair is standing on end, I look like a clown trying to control myself... Then I get up and walk away, and the bloody egg-timer on the screen is still there.

Nina Myskow

I wish to be cremated. One tenth of my ashes shall be given to my agent, as written in our contract.

Groucho Marx

Midlife is when the growth of the hair on our legs slows down. This gives us plenty of time to care for our newly acquired moustache.

Anon

I've gotten to the age where
I need my false teeth and
hearing aid before I can ask
where I left my glasses.

Anon

I would like to deny all allegations by Bob Hope that during my last game of golf I hit an eagle, a birdie, an elk and a moose.

Gerald Ford

The conception of two people
living together for 25 years
without having a cross word
suggests a lack of spirit only
to be admired in sheep.

Alan Patrick Herbert

Youth would be an ideal state
if it came a little later in life.

Herbert Asquith

Middle age is having a choice
of two temptations and
choosing the one that will get
you home earlier.

Dan Bennett

I wouldn't say her bathing suit was skimpy, but I've seen more cotton in the top of an aspirin bottle.

Henny Youngman

Instead of getting married again, I'm going to find a woman I don't like and just give her a house.

Rod Stewart

Bigamy is having one wife too many. Marriage is the same.

Oscar Wilde

I'd marry again if I found
a man who had 15 million
dollars, would sign over half
to me, and guarantee that
he'd be dead within a year.

Bette Davis

The Three Ages of Marriage:
20 is when you watch the TV
after. 40 is when you watch
the TV during. 60 is when
you watch the TV instead.

Anon